STILL MORE
CHURCH CHUCKLES

STILL MORE CHURCH CHUCKLES

by DICK HAFER

New Leaf Press

First printing: February 1997

ISBN: 0-89221-340-X

Please feel free to use these pages for your bulletins, fax messages, etc.

Dedication

Thanks to all of those who helped to come up with cartoon ideas for this, and my first two cartoon collections. They include: Marsha Davidson; Dick Wertz; Tom Wertz; and, of course, my wife and partner, Mary.

Thanks also to all of you who had the consumate good taste and highly developed sense of humor to buy *Church Chuckles* and *More Church Chuckles*. Without you, I'd be doing cartoons on the curb in front of my house — with a sign, "Will do cartoons for food."

And, to those who stood in the bookstore and enjoyed my cartoons without buying the books . . . PUT THIS BOOK DOWN, OR TAKE IT TO THE CASH REGISTER!

I thank you and my mortgage-holder thanks you.

These cartoons are not meant to make fun
of God's _church_ but to get us to laugh with each other
at the ways of God's _people_ . . . us.

The most effective ministers I've ever known,
all shared a vibrant sense of humor.

After all, who has more to be happy about than us?
I've read the back of the book . . . we win!

Always laugh when you can; it is cheap medicine..

— Lord George Noel Gordon Byron (1788–1824)

If you're not allowed to laugh in heaven, I don't want to go there.

— Martin Luther (1483–1546)

THERE! WE'RE DONE! I TOLD YOU THAT PHILIPPIANS WOULDN'T TAKE TOO LONG.

" . . . AND NOW, WITH AN OPPOSING VIEW. . . ."

THAT OUGHTA DO IT! THERE'S NO WAY THEY'LL KNOW IT'S A CHURCH!

DR. WARFIELD FOUND THAT THE MORE SERIOUSLY HE TOOK "POLITICAL CORRECTNESS," THE LESS HE HAD TO WORK WITH.

WE'VE MET SEVERAL TIMES NOW, MR HALLON, SO TONIGHT I'VE BROUGHT DEACON MONGO ALONG TO HELP YOU SEE THE LIGHT.

I THINK IT'S NICE THAT SINCE HE RETIRED, ANDY'S BEEN A VOLUNTEER HANDYMAN AT THE CHURCH!

THE TALL MEN ON THE BUILDING COMMITTEE NEVER CONSULTED THE WOMEN
WHEN PLANNING THE NEW KITCHEN.

THERE <u>ARE</u> SOME DOWNSIDES TO CHURCH FAMILY CAMPING.

SO NEVER GET INVOLVED IN A PRE-MARITAL INTIMATE RELATIONSHIP!
IT COULD LEAD TO... DANCING!

I'M AFRAID I'M GONNA GET THE FIRING SQUAD!

NO... IT DISTINCTLY SAYS "FIG."

YOU KNOW HOW YOU KEEP TEACHING ABOUT "DO UNTO OTHERS AS YOU WOULD HAVE THEM DO UNTO YOU"? WELL, WOULD YOU GIVE **YOURSELF** A REPORT CARD LIKE **THIS**?

THE CONGREGATION'S IDEA OF THE PERFECT PARSONAGE.

NO, I'M SORRY. PASTOR IS
OUT ON CALLS.

ISN'T IT NICE THAT THE PARSONAGE HERE AT OUR NEW CHURCH HAS SO MANY OF OUR FELLOW CHURCH MEMBERS AS NEIGHBORS?

THERE! LISTEN TO THAT FALWELL GUY! I DON'T KNOW WHERE YOU KIDS
GET THAT #!?#!&%! LANGUAGE YOU USE!!

I FIXED THAT LIGHT SWITCH, PASTOR. I LOVE HELPING OUT HERE AT CHURCH SINCE I RETIRED!

SO THANKS FOR COMING TONIGHT. MY BOOKS, RECORDS, AND TAPES ARE AVAILABLE AT THE BACK OF THE CHURCH. IN ADDITION, WE ARE OFFERING MY WIFE'S "VINEYARD" BRAND JAMS, JELLIES, AND RELISHES!

PASTOR, I'M SO PROUD THAT GRANDMA'S PRICELESS ANTIQUE DESK
WILL BE A PERMANENT PART OF THE CHURCH DECOR!

...AND THIS IS ONE OF THE MOST HOLY RELICS IN ALL CHRISTENDOM....
THIS IS ST. PAUL'S ACTUAL SAFETY RAZOR!

HIS PARENTS NEVER RETURNED FOR HIM.

AHA! A GUM WRAPPER!! *PROOF POSITIVE THAT KIDS HAVE NO PLACE IN CHURCH!!*

I KNOW... BUT THE WILL STATED THAT THE ONLY THING THE MONEY COULD BE USED FOR WAS A 25-FOOT, CIRCULAR STAINED GLASS WINDOW.

THE FAUCET BLEW OFF! HERE... HURRY UP! DAM UP THE FLOOD WITH DISH TOWELS!!
C'MON! DAM IT! **DAM IT! DAM IT!!**

BUT I'M NOT A SINNER! I'VE NEVER BOUGHT A REAL FUR COAT OR POLLUTED A STREAM!

HERE YOU ARE, LADIES! HOW DOES IT FEEL TO HAVE US HUSBANDS WAIT ON **YOU** FOR THE MOTHER'S DAY BANQUET?!!

PASTOR CARTWRIGHT IS A MASTER OF THE ALTAR CALL.

IT ALL STARTED WITH WHETHER I CORINTHIANS 13:13 SHOULD BE TRANSLATED AS "CHARITY" OR "LOVE" AND WENT DOWNHILL FROM THERE.

YEAH, IT *IS* IMPRESSIVE ... BUT WE'RE A **BAPTIST** CHURCH!

HI, MR. GERWIG. I'M BERNIE, FROM THE CHURCH "HELPING HAND COMMITTEE." THEY ASKED ME TO TAKE THIS MORNING'S ALTAR FLOWERS TO A SHUT-IN . . . AND I THOUGHT OF YOU.

BERNIE IS SENT TO PICK UP PIZZA FOR THE YOUTH GROUP.

THE TROUBLE WITH BEING THE FIRST GUY ON EARTH,
IS NOT HAVING ANYONE ELSE TO BLAME.

I NEED A NEW DRESS, ADAM.

WHAT'S A "DRESS"?

THIS DRIVER MUST BE THE SUNDAY SCHOOL'S PLAN FOR
GETTING US TO PRAY MORE OFTEN!

IT MIGHT HAVE BEEN BETTER TO LEAVE YOUR MOTHER AT HOME.

BILLY KIDWELL'S PRACTICAL JOKES HIT A NEW LOW WHEN THE NEW PULPIT ARRIVED.

WE'RE GOING BROKE WITH GLASS CLEANER BILLS!!

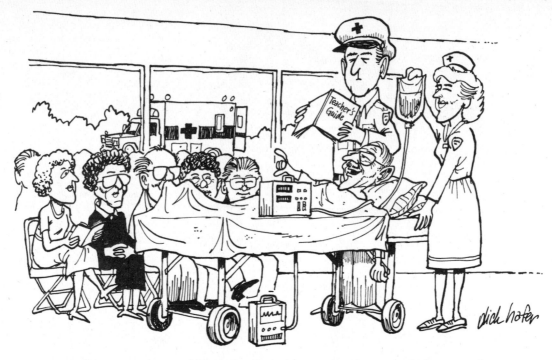

MR. TORKLESON HASN'T MISSED A DAY OF TEACHING THE
SENIOR SUNDAY SCHOOL CLASS IN OVER 32 YEARS.

IT WAS PROBABLY A MISTAKE TO HAVE THE "BLESSING OF THE PETS" AND THE LIGHTING OF THE CHRISTMAS TREE AT THE SAME SERVICE.

SO, WE'D LIKE TO THANK BROTHER HENDERSON FOR DONATING THIS BEAUTIFUL NEW PLEXIGLASS PULPIT.

I'M GONNA WIN THAT "BRING YOUR FRIENDS TO SUNDAY SCHOOL" CONTEST PRIZE **THIS** YEAR!

CAN WE PLEASE GET SOME VOLUNTEERS TO DO A LITTLE YARD WORK DURING THE JANITOR'S ABSENCE?

ONE OF THE MEMBERS OF THE WOMEN'S QUARTET WAS SICK THAT SUNDAY MORNING.

I WONDER WHY OUR CHURCH ISN'T GROWING?

IT'S THE LASTEST CONCEPT... "SKY BOXES" FOR THE BIGGEST CONTRIBUTORS.

YES, I'M SO PROUD. TWO YEARS AGO OUR PRISON MINISTRY FOLKS TOOK SOME OF MY LIVER & NOODLES TO THE JAIL. NOW, THE WARDEN HAS ME DO A LOT OF COOKING FOR THE PRISONERS! HE SAYS THAT REPEAT OFFENDERS ARE DOWN **37%** ... AND HE GIVES **ME** ALL OF THE CREDIT!

62

GREAT NEWS, GUYS! MRS. HANSEN TOLD TRUDY THAT
SHE'S **NOT** BRINGING THAT HORRIBLE LIVER AND
NOODLES CASSEROLE OF HERS TO THE DINNER!

I HOPE YOU'RE NOT TOO DISAPPOINTED, BUT I
BROUGHT SOMETHING NEW TO THE POTLUCK...
MY OWN, SPECIAL **LIVER CREAM PIE!**

MRS. HANSEN!! YOU KNOW THE HOSPITAL RULES! YOU'RE WELCOME ...BUT YOUR **FOOD** STAYS OUT!!

DADDY!! I THINK I HEAR A POLICE CAR SIREN! HIDE THE MANGER SCENE, QUICK!

NO... **YOU** ASK THEM WHAT CHURCH THEY'RE FROM.

TIMMY... WE'VE GOT TO TALK.

WELL, IT'S NICE TO SEE THAT CALVIN FINALLY GOT TO CHURCH
ON A DAY OTHER THAN CHRISTMAS OR EASTER.

ADAM... YOU WANT **THAT** FOR DINNER?!! OKAY... BUT I'LL HAVE BERRIES.

THE CHOIR DIRECTOR HAD SOME WEIRD IDEAS BEFORE...
BUT THIS EASTER CANTATA IS THE PITS!

PASTOR... I DON'T FEEL THAT YOU'RE TAKING OUR PROBLEM SERIOUSLY.

PASTOR ... WE'VE **GOT** TO GET AIR CONDITIONING FOR THE CHURCH!!

LAND SAKES, PASTOR! MY SON AND HIS FAMILY HAVE BEEN VISITING FOR TWO WEEKS AND THEY'RE TREATING ME LIKE A QUEEN! THEY WON'T LET ME LIFT A FINGER. . . . WOULD YOU BELIEVE WE'VE EATEN <u>EVERY SINGLE MEAL</u> AT RESTAURANTS?!!

THIS IS WONDERFUL, PASTOR! NOW THAT THE CHURCH PROVIDED YOU WITH A PORTABLE CELLULAR TELEPHONE, WE'LL **NEVER** BE OUT OF TOUCH WITH YOU!

MODERN EVANGELISM PACKAGED PROGRAMS TO "GROW YOUR CHURCH."

CHURCH MISSIONS COMMITTEE

YOU'RE FOREVER COMING BACK HERE AND BEGGING FOR YOUR MISSION! NEXT YOU'LL BE BELLYACHING 'CAUSE YOU HAVE NO FOOD! **WHERE'S YOUR FAITH, MAN?!!**

THE CHURCH COUNCIL THOUGHT THIS WOULD BOOST CONTRIBUTIONS.

THAT WAS A GOOD SUNDAY SCHOOL LESSON!
I'LL GIVE UP BROCCOLI AND SPINACH FOR LENT!

THE EARLY CHURCH IN AMERICA

WHEN THE AMISH GO BAD.

OOPS!

SO, IF ANYONE HERE KNOWS ANY REASON WHY THESE TWO SHOULD NOT BE. . . .

IT CERTAINLY IS NICE TO SEE OUR NEW PASTOR AND HIS FAMILY MOVING IN. HMMM ... YOU <u>DO</u> LIKE FINE QUALITY FURNITURE, DON'T YOU? YOU REALLY SHOULD KEEP THIS JEWELRY IN A SAFER PLACE. WE LADIES OF THE CHURCH WILL BE GLAD TO HELP YOU ARRANGE THINGS.

THIS IS THE FIRST WEDDING YOU'VE CATERED, I PRESUME?

HARRY . . . COME TO BED, DEAR. I'M SURE IF THE RAPTURE OCCURS OVERNIGHT, YOU'LL WAKE UP FOR IT.

HI! I'M FROM RIVERDALE CHURCH, AND I'M HERE TO . . . OH, OH.

SOMETHING'S GOT TO BE DONE ABOUT THE TRASH ON CABLE TV!
EVERY WEEK I'M SUBJECTED TO HOUR AFTER HOUR OF TERRIBLE FILTH!

HURRY UP! GO GET SOME MORE GOODIES! WE MAY RAISE ALL OF THE MONEY WE NEED FOR THE NEW CHURCH KITCHEN, IN THE NEXT FEW MINUTES!!

THAT'S A HEART-WRENCHING STORY! HERE, TAKE THIS TRACT ... IT'LL SOLVE ALL OF YOUR PROBLEMS.

OH, OH!

*I KNOW THAT IT'S A LITTLE EARLY FOR OUR COUNSELING SESSION, PASTOR...
BUT THERE ARE SOME THINGS I NEED TO TELL YOU ABOUT.*

THE MISSIONARY'S FIRST U.S. FURLOUGH IN 14 YEARS.

THE NIGHT THE CAKE DELIVERY MAN MADE A SERIOUS MISTAKE.

THE NIGHT THE CAKE DELIVERY MAN MADE A SERIOUS MISTAKE.

BOY! OUR BUS MINISTRY IS *REALLY* WORKING!!

THANKS! YOUR GROUP HAS FINALLY SOLVED MY GAMBLING PROBLEM!
... I BET YOU 100 BUCKS I NEVER HAVE TO COME BACK!

YOU CAN BET YOUR LIFE THAT NEXT YEAR WE'LL TAKE A LOT CLOSER LOOK AT THE SHOW BOOTH LAYOUT!!

THE EARLY CHURCH IN AMERICA

THE FIRST YOUTH GROUP HAYRIDE.

I THINK I JUST DISCOVERED WHY WE HAVEN'T SEEN MR. KELCHER IN CHURCH FOR THE PAST COUPLE OF YEARS.

OUR **THEOLOGY?** WELL ... WE BELIEVE IN GOD AND STUFF LIKE THAT. LET ME TELL YOU ABOUT THE <u>GREAT</u> INTEREST GROUPS WE HAVE FOR EVERYONE!

IT'S OUR WAY OF MAKING SURE THAT YOU'RE GREETED PROPERLY.

THE *RABBIT DIED?!* BUT I'M *90 YEARS OLD!!*

SO THEN, FATHER MURPHY, I COULDN'T CONTROL MYSELF, SO I....

WELL!! I MUST SAY, **THAT** WAS CERTAINLY AN UNUSUAL BLESSING!

ONE THING FOR SURE . . . ONCE THE WATER RECEDES, WE'RE NOT GOING TO HAVE ANY SHORTAGE OF FERTILIZER FOR THE NEW CROPS!

YEAH . . . WE **DID** USE THE LOW BIDDER FOR OUR NEW STEEPLE. WHY DO YOU ASK?

...AND THEN, ON THE 38TH DAY OF OUR HOLY LAND TRIP....

MMMM!! LIVER 'N' NOODLES!! MY FAVORITE! MY DEAR,
LATE WIFE USED TO MAKE THIS FOR ME ONCE A WEEK!

YOU'VE BEEN A BAD BOY AGAIN, MR. DEAVERS. LET'S GO BACK TO THE HOME.
HOW DID YOU PICK THE LOCK THIS TIME?

NO...I'M SORRY...YOU'RE IN THE "SMOKING SECTION."

THE EARLY CHURCH IN AMERICA.

O-62...OOPS! WRONG GROUP....

THIS IS GETTING OUTTA HAND!

THE GENEROUS DONATION OF A NEW PASTOR'S AUTOMOBILE, BY MR. WILSON, *DID* HAVE ITS DOWNSIDE.

THE NEXT ORDER OF BUSINESS IS TO ARRANGE FOR A
NEW CHURCH VEHICLE FOR THE YOUTH PASTOR.

122

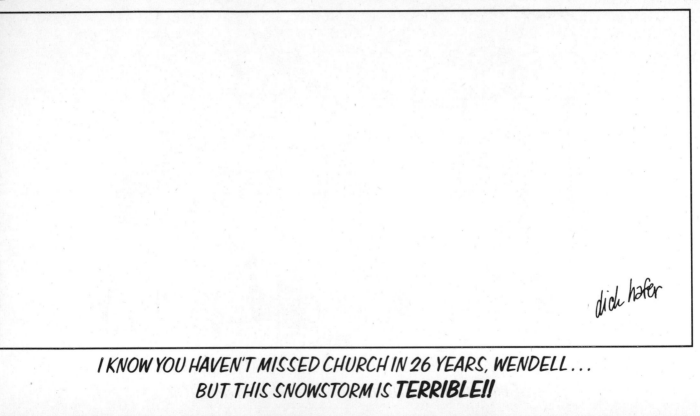

I KNOW YOU HAVEN'T MISSED CHURCH IN 26 YEARS, WENDELL...
BUT THIS SNOWSTORM IS **TERRIBLE!!**

IN RETROSPECT... IT MAY HAVE BEEN BETTER TO HOLD THE MORTGAGE-BURNING SERVICE **OUTSIDE.**

SO, THIS RIDICULOUS IDEA OF A "RAPTURE" IS JUST ANOTHER BIBLICAL MYTH, WHICH
...*WHERE'D EVERYBODY GO?!!*

FOR CRYIN' OUT LOUD, CYNTHIA!! WE'RE LATE FOR CHURCH! GET BACK IN
— I'LL **BUY** YOU SOME APPLES!!

GET ME THE PASTORAL CALL COMMITTEE!!

Also available...

...from your favorite
Christian bookstore